Tess, the Best Dog

By Sascha Goddard

Dogs are the best pets.

Dogs like to have fun with us.

Tess is my dog!

Dogs can jog with you.

Boss can jog up a hill.

This is fun, Boss!

You can toss stuff for dogs.

Dogs are not dull.

Dogs can run.

They can hop up and up!

Go, Cass!

Some dogs sit still
with no fuss.

Let's sit, Russ.

But dogs can be bad, too!

Dogs can mess stuff up.

Look at this mess!

7

It's less fun if a dog is ill.

I will hug and kiss you, Moss.

Dogs are top pets!

Tess is my best pal!

CHECKING FOR MEANING

1. What animal does the author think is the best pet? (*Literal*)

2. What do dogs do that is bad? (*Literal*)

3. Why is it less fun if your dog is ill? (*Inferential*)

EXTENDING VOCABULARY

dull	What is the meaning of *dull* in this book? What other words have a similar meaning? E.g. boring, uninteresting. Is there another meaning of this word? I.e. not shiny.
fuss	What is a *fuss*? Do you ever make a fuss? What do you do? What are other words with a similar meaning? E.g. trouble, bother, worry.
less	What does *less* mean in this text? Explain to students that it means not as much, or fewer. So, if something is *less* fun, what does this mean? What other words in the book rhyme with *less*?

MOVING BEYOND THE TEXT

1. Do you think dogs or cats make better pets? Why?

2. What are the names of some dog breeds you know?

3. If you could have a dog, what breed would you like? Why?

4. What do you have to do to care for a dog?

SPEED SOUNDS

| ff | ll | ss | zz |

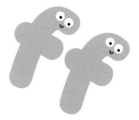

PRACTICE WORDS

Tess Boss hill Moss

toss stuff dull miss

Jess fuss will Cass

still Russ mess ill

kiss less